Primary Sources

for Leslie —

Poems

Neighbor, lover of dogs,
musician, friend.
with much affection
Ann

Ann Staley

Ann Staley

Booktrope Editions
Seattle WA
2011

Cover Picture: Judy Teufel

Cover Design: Dana Sullivan

ISBN 978-1-935961-23-9

DISCOUNTS OR CUSTOMIZED EDITIONS MAY BE AVAILABLE
FOR EDUCATIONAL AND OTHER GROUPS BASED ON BULK
PURCHASE.

For further information please contact info@booktrope.com

Library of Congress Control Number: 2011912899

For Elizabeth Devine Staley
1917-1990

Acknowledgments

For teachers, Winifred Kitchen and Eleanor Shaffner of Progress Elementary School; Ron Zeigler, Susquehanna Township Junior High School, and later of the Advanced American Literature class, and for Pete Fackler, faculty advisor, whom everyone loved. For my Green Acres friends Bob, Betty, and Jim Tarman and Pete Zirilli; for Cindy Fendrich and junior and senior high school friends David Isele, Kathy DeWalt Kreider, Jerry Kreider, Jim Miller, a nuclear engineer who prefers non-fiction, and for David Stinson who suggested the title for this collection. For Judy Lehrman, Cynthia Melman, Barbara Reiter who "danced to the music" and read books and knew college would save us. For all the lifeguards and swim coaches at Colonial Country Club, for Bob and Steve Schreckengaust, and Larry Hetzel who carried me to the club-house after the diving board accident; to Ron Benoit, Paul Ratowsky and Ed Mulholland, wherever they are; to Ellen Myers, and the whole Kappa Kappa Gamma clan who elected me President one year. To Peace Corps friends, Richard Becker, Richard Mermey and to Beth and Len Eisenhood; to some very special students – Richard Schlecter, Tess Thompson, Jenny Fowler, Darcy Martin, Eric Pugh, Gary Plant and the entire Honors Class, because some students are as sustaining as mentors. For Aubrey and Kelly and Bill Robbins. For many mentors at Bard College including Paul Connolly, Theresa Vilardi, Rob Whittemore, Sharyn Layfield; at Lewis & Clark, Elizabeth Beverly, Diane McDevitt, and Kim Stafford; and at Stanford University, Larry Cuban and Elliot Eisner. Also for Nels Thompson, Florence Walraven, Joan Flora, Cindy Graff and Jeff Mitchell, extraordinary colleagues at Philomath High School. For Victor who tried to hold fast and for Michael who apologized with a handshake, because everything that happens to us is carried along forever in our hearts. For my Corvallis writing group, Women (Still) Writing, and for the Rose City Writing Group; for the Pretzels and the Sunnyside Writers, Steve and Rachel, cheering all the way. Every member of a writing group, in my case ages forty to eighty, brings her/his own wise words, shared by all. For Darryla and Dan, from Gold Beach onward, and for Michael Malan who took me seriously as a poet. For Peter Sears and Anita Helle who know how to celebrate successes and who quietly love their friends. For Sheila Shafer and Ann and Erik Mueller of Eugene. For Ashland friends, Jeff LeLande, Anne and Stew McCollom, Judy Drais and Judy Howard, for Sabra and Dave Hoffman, Susan and Dwight Roper, Cathy and John Schleining; for Sylvia and Sandy Goodman; and for Nancy Joachim who arrived, by surprise, just the other day. For all the Trustees and Friends of William Stafford, and for Dorothy Stafford especially. For my neighbors, Carolyn

LaTierra, who gardens in the rain, for Charla Van Koten, in-depth listener and her wonderful husband Dr. Stan Nudelman, and for Barb Lachenbruch, working on trees. For Leslie Wood and Cheryl Rosine. For Steven Black, lawyer, who took big risks and lives with injustice, and for 'his' Susan. For the homeless men "on the bench" every day, and for those down at the Post Office - you and the memory of my younger brother, Tom, keep me honest. For Patti White and Rick Wallace, for Florence Walraven and Dick Shirmer, for Dave Lacka and Ted Norton. For long-time friends Alan Koch and Grace LeBlanc, Elaine Barker and Doug Cortrecht, Kay and Norm Johnson, and newer, but no less dear friends, Jack and Nancy Fischer, Drew Myron and David Riesek, Erika Schoell and Meghan Caughey. For the Menucha 2010 "Refuge" writers – never to be forgotten our week together. For Jane's Book Club readers and great gals. For Be and Jack Herrera and for Bill and Sue and Paige Shumway. For all of you who've shared the Rogue River, and especially for Holly Mayer and Ken Kondeziela who twice shared Paradise with all their friends, and for James Mayer on guitar & computer security. For Jack Wolcott and Sandy Smith, co-owners of Grass Roots Independent Book Store, and who do so much for artists and writers in our community; for their book store manager, Tiffany Jordan, and staff, Sarah Norek and Michael Beilstein; and for Lynn Russell, friend and artist of Satsuma Press; For the Corvallis Arts Center, Sara Swanberg, Hester Coucke, Joni King, and all the volunteers just around the corner. For private school extraordinaire, Catlin Gabel, and for the teachers I know there, Tom Tucker, Hanna Whitehead, and Judy Teufel, retired teacher and artist with a van that holds everything one could ever need for teaching a workshop, repairing a house or taking a road trip. For the Oregon Writing Project, thirty years of teachers-teaching-teachers! For Claira Woolley, a great-grandmother and head of her clan, and for my niece Liz Staley, with a book of her own. For my cousin Betsy Anne Devine Gremp and her retired Admiralty of a husband Bob Gremp. For my sister-in law, Wendy Cloyd, a dear friend and a beautiful blonde. Finally for my older brother Jed, aunt, Anne Devine and grandparents, Thomas and Sarah Devine, and for my parents, Edwin Lewis Staley and Elizabeth Kane Devine Staley. And certainly for my Encouragers: Betty and Bill Martin who in a time of terrible trouble sent me one word on a torn piece of paper —courage! For publishers Katherine Sears and Kenneth Shear who said, "We want to publish your poems." For the Healers: Jane Megard, Dr. Sang Ly Montage, Dr. Beth Laurensen, Dr. Susan Ahart, and for Jerri Elliot Otto, editor extraordinaire. And especially, for Courtney Cloyd, light of my life.

Contents

Singer

Walking in One Direction

Resolution

Night rain sings against the roof
pounds its rhythm faster than a cat's purring heart.
Memory floods the closing day.

The surface of the swollen river, a gray convexity
water rushes the bridge pilings, folds itself around them,
heads with the gradient, downstream.

Naked apple branches, brushstrokes on sky,
while the Sweet Gum holds her last golden letters.
They will fall, we know, just before the crocus.

This new year, more words and light,
old fires, new fruit,
a path opening toward trees, toward water.

If It's Not Too Dark
Hafiz sends his wishes

Go, get, try.
Say something.

Exercise.

Attempt (something real).

Take, pour, gaze.
Play, extend, sing.
Let them
toast, love.

Love.

Stop reading.
Understand Him.

Jump, wave, threaten, and warn.

My heart can no longer
live
without Him.

Sing, O My Tongue, the Glorious
(Pange Lingua Gloriosi)

1.

Long before she
discovered unlined
composition books &
fine-point Pilot pens;
before she watched her
left-handed, botoxed cursive
evolve toward print
resembling Hokusai's spring rain;
and even before,
the dry-hot Ashland August
when a voice emerged
full-blown, bossy,
still second-guessing,
she'd loved the whispered,
drone of language,
the Catholic Mass,
its mystery mixed with incense
and improbable faith,
its *Mea Culpa*,
its *Gloria!*

2.

She knew wild violets,
corn rows surrounding Madar's barn,
the Negro Cemetery unlocked,
neighbor twins & an Irish Setter,
the girl whose parents divorced,
Nonna Mazzi tending a front-yard garden –
tomatoes and beans, squash, eggplant –
shocking in the suburbs
where canned goods, barbecues and cigarettes
proved we'd won a war.

At Six, Pedaling
- for Jed

No school, not even an alarm clock buzz; no demanding call to a poached-egg breakfast; no braids pulled tight across the scalp; no plaid ribbons. Saturday opens like a book I've chosen myself – *The Boxcar Children, Mary Queen of Scots.* Our parents sleep late while we devour bowls of Corn Flakes and sugary raisins in front of the T.V. We play records, begin Monopoly games that will last until Sunday, argue about chores. Such flannel-pj'd-independence taking messages – *Call Aunt Peg. Tom will stop by before dinner. Mrs. Zirilli needs the mower.* – trading the dozen brown eggs delivered by Mr. McElhinny for two quarters Dad has stacked on his folded white handkerchief. Ike and J. Edgar, Marilyn and Joe, Walt Disney and Elvis sleep late too. We pack peanut butter crackers and Juicy Fruit, head out on Schwinns. South on 31st Street, we pedal toward Madar's dusty pond, it's cool, gray-green water surrounded by dry grasses.

Wild Violets

Below the ravine and Mercy Crest Convent, I gather wild violets. Lime green strands of algae undulate in the water. Soft water sounds, leaves dapple summer light, cool moist air tastes like damp earth. I'm crouched above the stream sporting wet navy tennis shoes. And I'm thirteen, trying to escape the suburbs that surround the ravine, the ranch houses built after World War II and carved out of Madar's Farm, escape as well from the house on the corner of 31st and Penbrook Avenue. I walked to Progress Elementary School and will walk to the Junior High school when the summer has passed. I'm proudly sporting braces and choosing electives to fill in around my post-Sputnik-college-track science and math classes. I struggle with algebra and love literature and writing. I'm too tall, have too many freckles and too many feelings. I know these things but can't do anything about them. I've taught my older brother to slow dance and jitterbug in the living room, discovered Bob Dylan by reading *Time Magazine*. I secretly play with dolls, but also listen to the radio at night, letting Johnny Mathis and The Four Tops lull me to sleep. My body is strong and beautiful, but I also know it will be years before anyone else will see it. I'm a competitive swimmer with crushes on all the college-age lifeguards. They are very kind to me, and the one of them who is a young woman confides, "You're going to love college when you get there." I think to myself, "Only five more years," an eternity when you're thirteen. This is the journey, isn't it, through adolescence – that foreign country.

You Stayed
 - *for Robert Tarman*

You lived east on Progress Avenue with your twin sister, Betty, your older brother. We all played together for years, on jungle gyms, roller skates, on bicycles. You were quiet, shy, but later I realized you had been watching me all along. Noticing, really, admiring. You stayed, as expected, in Harrisburg. I went west, the wind in my dark hair, and didn't see you again for thirty years.

At the reunion, walking across the dance floor in the same direction, heading for our seats at small round tables, you brought me to a halt by saying my name aloud, the name no one else alive used any more: "Ann Ellen," you said, and then, "Boo" ('Boo' shortened from 'Beautiful,' shortened from 'Precious Beautiful') Then you took my hand in yours searching for the wedding ring. You held it, examining the diamond, trying to figure if it was a wedding diamond or just a pretty ring. I got the message directly from your heart and said, "You're too late, Bob, you needed to have asked me a long time ago."

We exchanged a couple of letters after that, West Coast to East Coast. We sent old photos of ourselves as school kids, as neighbors. I invited you to visit Oregon, encouraged you to marry the woman you'd been dating, to adopt her children. You did, but didn't tell me. What you did tell me was, "I knew you'd become a writer. I knew you'd do something interesting with your life."

And then you died last Christmas - a heart attack. Your twin sister died within six months, before I could write to tell her about loving you. And so it was your older brother, Jim, who met me for dinner when I visited in the fall. We both cried. I told him everything, sent a copy of your letter to me, illegible lawyer handwriting. He told me you'd tried sobriety, nearly died in the hospital, then went on drinking, an alcoholic-in-hiding. He also told about the number of murder trials you'd taken on as a P.D. – that you'd won acquittal for your client in each case. And about the time you stood on the desk in your office shouting, "I'm taking a year off. I'm driving to the Pacific." We laughed until we cried. Then I put my head down right beside an empty salad plate and cried in earnest. This early, lost love, feeling as deep and wide as the river that flows through our hometown.

In my study I watched the video shown at the Fundraiser, in honor of your work. The clients you took who couldn't pay, the ones who could but didn't, those folks who are so often invisible, but who need lawyerly advice and assistance – immigrants, the elderly, non-English speakers, the abused, the homeless, those people whom many feel don't deserve rights, including the right-to-counsel. I see you accept an award from N.O.W. without standing on your desk, smile into the camera and say, "Thank you." I remembered your voice then, the man who said my name on the dance floor. I miss it still.

Heading South, Lanes Shift Ahead

Phone message recorded in the basement, ends, "I love you."

At the French Bakery paying for lemonade, the cashier
cups her hand, presses the dollar against her open palm.

At the Market, noticing the high price of spring artichokes
the bin stocker touches her shoulder, says they grew behind his
        grandfather's trailer.

Yearling eating shoulderside stubble along the Interstate,
abandoned shoes below the overpass at Riddle.

Near Canyonville: Lanes Shift Ahead Above moving traffic
a water tower, tucked into a forested hill, fog curling along the crest.

Metamorphic rock-fall and catchment near Quines Creek.
At the roadside rest stop, sign on a rusted out Chevy: Out of Gas,
        Please Help

Stage Road, Smith Hill, Sexton Pass, silver sedan with snow tires
rolls toward spring, Valley pear trees in bloom.

Walking in One Direction

I half-touch
my mother's death
every day,
a stroke at 73.
I thought it was the drinking
and smoking.
But my doctor tells me,
"It's about the heart itself."
Not the metaphorical one,
dear poet."
She says after listening,
"Has anyone ever told you
about your irregular heart beat,
those premature flutterings, PVC's
Two normal beats, and then ...?"
On the sonogram
I watch this magic muscle
do its irregular thing,
so strong and sure,
then the flutter
I sometimes feel
when I embrace a friend,
or with Courtney –
late, autumn darkness coming on.
If genetics has its way with me,
I have more years without meds,
and like everyone else,
a 50-50 chance.

Looking at the Susquehanna

How full of movement was the night sky
and, yes, I was completely loved.
I remember it all —
noticing the details,
how hair curls out close to the scalp
the confluence, the flowing together, flowing North —
as though it were yesterday.

And this too —
something unspeakable had happened.

At some point this poem will hold us more easily.

Looking Up-River, August

There's a dove, somewhere cooing,
a flag at half-mast.
A young man tends a burn pile,
leaves from last night's,
once-in-twenty-one-years' storm,
        (lightning)
        (hail, too)
says Ray, the neighbor with three earrings.

Last night, too,
in utter darkness,
a raccoon tussled with a river otter
who slipped away downstream
just as three more coons appeared and swam
in front of the deck.
A territorial issue, a smallish war.
But that was last night.

This evening, sun setting out beyond "the Sisters"
those girls still holding snow patches
on their northern flanks.

With candlelight, wine, blankets,
we watch the day-blind stars come on.
The Dipper, North Star, a bright and visible planet:
Near this moving water, I am an innocent.

A Yacht

A yacht, a retirement community at Neskowin.
My preparation – white wine.
Day lilies are nothing but aggressive.

Paula on her bicycle at First Presbyterian,
the last to leave the concert or the class,
smiling her secret smile, moving hesitantly.

Who cares about us, the retired, the women,
the disabled, the mothers and daughters,
those who want "Peace Now"

those who honor the natural world,
who honor filaments, tendrils,
the self-spun hope we make in this room,

with candle light, scent of lilies,
a guitar soloist purposefully fading away.
We are as profoundly silenced as Sappho,

but our words and our stance will survive us.
Together we mark the arc of justice bending
toward the Gulf Coast, toward the slums

surrounding Mumbai, the World Cup finale
in South Africa, watched by billions on
generator TV, people without potable water

or transportation more sophisticated than the bicycle.
This rant is the subconscious revealing itself,
the stones Virginia placed in her pockets,

the truth and the consequences. The dream
of the dream or the Now that includes us all,
our missing mothers, fathers, siblings,

and including our loves and our poems.

Is this the end of something or simply
a mid-June evening, breezes and blue sky,

the promise of summer singing its sweet blessing.

First Kisses
You kissed me once, and now I wait for more.
          Elizabeth Alexander

I was older than fourteen, Elizabeth, but mine were sweet, too, at the Drive-In movies, all one summer, Paul and I deliriously entwined front seat and back seat, such sweet kisses and touching. If he'd asked me, I probably would have, you know, "gone further," so thank god he didn't. Off to University of Iowa mid-summer, we wrote our version of love letters. I'm sure I sent poems by Emily and Walt. Three times later in my life, Paul stepped in out of nowhere with his earnest love for me.   First rescue at Penn State - requested on the East Coast - and twice more in Ashland - all happenstance on the West Coast.

One winter weekend Paul arrived in State College. I have no idea where he stayed or why I needed him, That weekend we attended the women's basketball game, the men's basketball game, a wrestling event, a Nittany Lions-hosted league final, and Ravi Shankar. Paul took me out for lunches, dinner, though I don't remember eating. No drinking, of course. We weren't "legal" in PA. Then he flew back to Iowa via our hometown.

Final rescue, Paul is 28 and drives into Ashland in a vintage, pale pink Cadillac convertible. He's visiting from Venice, CA where he's invested in oil wells (I am not making this up). and selling his paintings on the boardwalk. He and his brother have just been paid a great deal of money to create a 67' x 103 ' portrait of Cassius Clay, of "Dance like a butterfly, sting like a bee" fame. I am a weeping, broken-hearted wreck. Paul takes me to see Woody Allen's "Bananas," in the middle of the day, and where laughing out loud, the goofy hilarity, begin my healing. I trusted his care and entrusted myself to his kindness then and again and again.

Acts of Contrition

Pierce Thou, my flesh with Thy fear.
Psalm 118

The body itself is a screen to shield and reveal
the light that's blazing inside your presence.
Rumi

Raised in the Roman Catholic Church -
St. Margaret Mary's, Harrisburg Diocese -
the Sisters of Mercy taught us:
Everything is a sin.
Nothing you'd consider pleasurable permitted.
Third scoop of French Vanilla Häagen-Dazs,
the sin of gluttony.
Confess that.
First boyfriend kisses, mortal sins.
Confess every one of them, and
time spent in the back seat of the Mustang, too.
Looking into the mirror,
at my own absolutely beautiful-15-year-old body,
I needed Rumi,
but had instead the *Saint Pius X, Daily Missal:*
I thought sadly,
No one will see this for decades.
Even thinking that, *One more sin to confess.*

The Proper of the Saints

St. Lucy, Virgin, Martyr
St Eusebius, Bishop,Martyr
St. Blaise, Bishop, Martyr
St. Adrew Corsini, Bishop, Confessor
St. Agatha, Virgin, Martyr
$N = 5$,
a small sample,
but I cannot avoid noticing
that the women are virgin martyrs
and the men hold high office in the Church.

The Proper of the Saints extends from November 27
through November 26 of the following year in
the Roman Catholic Church.

Heading North
  - *with thanks to the Walin' Jennys*

Hawk shadows cross the road,
head full of words, no useful expression.

Worn-out daffodils along the Interstate,
though the moon could take us to morning.

Winter brush piles, Swift Transportation in the slow lane.
Next Exit - Enchanted Forest.

The guest speaker nervously holds his breath,
his passenger breathes deeply, addicted to "No."

Red lights flashing, emergency copter descends.
The notebook carries every warning against this love.

She comes back broken, *in want of mercy,*
ten thousand memories sticking to her skin.

Late Night Reading

The man looks back, speaks in the past tense.
The woman walks in the present tense, imagines the future.

The man remembers an osprey, lake trout, deer, tanagers —
and a puma.
The woman notices the waves carving a rock channel,
the starfish, anemones, crabs, crows and gulls.

The man says of the trout, "It could breathe, but never be water."
And the woman answers, "Stay wet and dead, you live."

The puma poses a question — and answers it — for the man;
The woman asks and answers her own question:
I'll be a starfish when this channel's finally cut.

The reader moves with each of them
from tidal pool to high rocky outcrop.
She wonders what she should know,
what she should take with her for the drive north:
Her nerves hunger to be trembling. Stone is nothing.
Deer nibble at the edges of the forest. Their night is water, day is air.
I'll kiss a rock hard, I'll feel like beadwork.
The soul has wings. Everything travels with me.

Getting To The Island

At the back door on Church Street
a note reads, "Her breathing has changed."

Driving I-5, eating sandwiches & listening to Yo-Yo Ma,
we pass the site of the nuclear reactor.

Exit 266, one way on Olive – asphalt, abandoned
Safeway carts, trash containers filled & waiting.
.
Freud reported that when speaking of a wedding
many clients unknowingly substituted the word funeral.

On the ferry headed north and west, the geologist remarks,
"From the sky these ridges are marked by glacial striations."

In the blue kitchen, morning sunlight, blackberries.
In the distant water, boats bob and jostle with the wind.

Somewhere near the dessert table, she remembers
the Greek poet's counsel: *Coming as far as this is not little.*

Dynamite

Carl's boss, Keith, embezzled one.point.two million.
He's serving 10 big ones, but Carl is still mad.

The embezzler's bank account was named:
Keith Nelson Doing Business as the School Board Commission.

Craig owns KFCs all over town, and said once,
"Fifty percent of my employees are stealing from me,

but I still love lawn chairs and Budweiser."
First think and then act is a wise saying of the Orient,

but obviously neither Carl's former boss
nor small businessman Craig is reading from the Tao.

I have faith in all things not said, Rilke writes in German,
and I think of my classroom harassers in whom I had so much faith,

the University protocol I followed, the Dean who held the evidence,
the University official who said, "Trust me."

When the official findings surfaced twenty days late,
they were summarized: "There were no violations."

My friend says, "I'm obsessive about not being obsessive."
I say, "Commence with out-of-control Post-Menopausal Zest,

fireworks, passion — and if nothing else works —
then dynamite.

Tensaku

It is a life lesson no middle child ever seeks
which makes it, of course, a necessary one.

Parents in the next world, brothers variously lost,
Pen-In-Left-Hand stranded near the Pacific.

Sweet and smart, the younger, lost to drugs & a roller-coaster
life of crisis, dies alone, a "John Doe" on the streets.

The older, "golden," gone-away, admired and loved,
makes it clear some words cannot be forgiven.

One, buried ashes in Pennsylvania's limestone soil.
One bicycling in Southern California.

What tangle of judgment, mistaken choices, karma,
made this bed of nails? Which way to resolution?

She eats local foods, pledges PBS, weeps for road kill,
hands change to homeless men outside the PO, along the river.

tensaku is the haiku word for "poetic ending"

Siblings
  - for Tom & Jed

That it will never come again
is what makes life so sweet. E.D.

After our mothers and fathers
disappear to the other side of life's veil,
our siblings become primary witnesses
to the arc of our lives.
They remember nicknames
and tantrums, polio shots,
school uniforms,
Bobby and Betty, the twins up the street,
the black Cocker Spaniel hit by a car.
They bought Cokes at Dad's gas station,
played pinball machines instead of
attending *Catechism* classes.
They remember the train station
in that coal town back east,
grandmother waving goodbye.

We rely on these sisters, these brothers,
to carry their memories and memories of us
forward to the next Thanksgiving or ravioli
party – to the next wedding or funeral.

We trust them to forget the ways
we may have failed them, or at least
forgive us our busy lives,
our need for solitude and white wine.

When they leave us,
we miss them like the body's
necessary second lung.
We miss their words, the sounds
of their breath and laughter,
the ways they taunted, teased,
reasoned, questioned – needed us.

But there they are in the photographs (& in dreams),
eating strawberries at your sixth birthday party.
You stand beside them at graduation.
They have your brown eyes, that east coast accent,
and you both look like your mother,
Christmas morning, 1954.
You have carried each other
long-distance, and just across town,
in wordless silence, in joy.
You carry each other — still.

Ann Staley

How to Keep On Standing

You need a pet for petting
and because that cat needs you,
thinks you're his cat mother.
And a neighbor or two who
notice you're up late, drinking too much,
and if it's summer, over-hear heated
conversation in the driveway.
A lover, a spouse who stays because,
like the cat, he is loyal beyond
human understanding, and through
verbal abuse or depression, if
either one, or both, are part
of the "shew," as Ed Sullivan used to call it.

And you need the other neighbor,
who didn't realize you had
trouble, that you worked as a professional
outside your home.
When you go over
with a glass of wine in your hand,
the third glass of the evening,
she tells her own story of harassment,
a student who wrote on a returned
paper, "I can't read your handwriting."

And to follow *that* conversation,
one more glass of wine, alone,
in your kitchen wondering,
if all this alcohol might
put you to sleep forever
when combined with a half
of a sleeping pill. "We'll see,"
you think to yourself as you swallow.

And then you need the morning,
gray clouds and rain,

waking from dark dreams, crying
to yourself as your local NPR
hosts an hour-long interview with
the nation's Poet Laureate who
reads "At the Cancer Clinic."

Not so. Not so.
You begin the day with the damned
interview, but turn the radio off
mid-sentence and wander toward
the front of the house, following
the fierce steaming scent of caffeine
to which you add half and half,
and sugar. Who cares? Who's counting?
And your dear husband says,
"I hoped you weren't listening."

You realize this is what Dante wrote
about all those centuries ago, in
Italian, and with all the translations
following, year after year, as though
no one else knew about the rings,
hadn't heard the grown-ups screaming,
begging for water, in the Sunday Catechism
film-strip Sister Margaret Mary showed
one morning, showed to those not attending
the Catholic school. And, that terrible
dilemma: *Only Catholics go to Heaven.*
You cried for all of one summer about
your father and your Nana, good people,
who would be screaming for water from
hell.

Instead of attempting conversions, you
became a risk-taker, building little
camp-fires in an empty field several blocks
from your home in Green Acres.
You stole a lipstick from a girlfriend's mother's
green glass dish – Coral Pink, you think now –
and later had to return it after your mother's
hysterical accusations, guilt-trip, and
humiliation. You were wrong,
you knew that, but nobody tried to figure
out "why" would someone like Ann Ellen
do this? What's going on with our girl?

In fact, you remember too clearly, the cool,
gray afternoon of the incident. Your mother's
hysteria and shame. You looked across the
porch and thought, "This is someone to whom
you must never reveal a problem. Solve
everything yourself." And mostly you did.

Including the illegal abortion in Baltimore.
You were 20. It was the summer of riots
and burning buildings in both D.C. and
Baltimore. You were picked up by a taxi
at midnight, from a downtown hotel,
collected by a driver wearing sun glasses,
and with a group of five or six women
delivered to a house in the suburbs.

The nurses and the doctors wore sunglasses,
spoke in cool, neutral voices. You wept until the
moment you fell into the deep sleep provided
by sodium pentathol. Your mother never knew.

You were ashamed, filled with guilt, but very
glad you weren't having a baby, abandoning
a college education. And the child would
be middle-aged now. You'd be a grandmother.
And maybe still married to your college lover
who was charming, sweet, a womanizer.

So many secrets. So much to solve secretly.
Was this a kind of "standing up?"
Only a lawyer or a theologian could say.
Your job is to resolve it, say it all
in this — confession

.

Begins With Seeing

November Ghazal

The only thing I know is the insensible
light disappearing at dusk.

Somehow in the blaze of the fire's flame
I remember my father's hands.

Tell me why a stranger's face on the street,
holds my attention, makes me wonder.

Have we all agreed about falling snow,
this white sky dropping is peace on earth?

No one alive now remembers my arrival,
daughter born with eyes open to summer.

It's all right if the melancholy oboe sings all night.
It's all right if geese rest in gray rows of field stubble.

Some Masters say we are all wounded here.
Ann, your wounds are messages from Paradise.

Portrait
- in memoriam, Elizabeth Kane Devine

For most of one year
I watched you watch yourself
in the vanity mirror,
cigarette burning in an ash-tray,
north light flooding the room,
your face.
The light revealed the soft down on your cheeks,
(and my own downy face seemed beautiful).
Eyebrow pencil and foundation make-up,
if you were preparing for an evening out.
Dior Red lipstick,
dark brown hair in a French twist.
One time, a black straw hat with a peony,
another time the ochre wool coat
you designed and sewed in the basement.
You were a beauty, "set the fashion standard,"
a Jackie Bouvier Kennedy
before anyone knew her name.

My Father's Cars

My dad "came from nothing,"
the last of 8 children,
descendants of South Mountain
Baptists, a Christian community
near Mount Alto, at the very center
of Pennsylvania.
No car whatsoever.
So later when he lived in a Harrisburg mansion,
he was able to move from longing
to his life-long affair with cars.
Nothing in high school, of course,
but after college, yes.
A procession of them beginning with
Chevrolets. (His eldest sister was married
into the first Chevy dealership in town.)

After the war
he switched brands, not of cigarettes
(a Lucky-Striker all his life)
but of automobiles.
And so the Fords:
A pale green Fairlane,
a red and white Fairlane 500,
the second Mustang sold in Harrisburg
(black with red leather interior),
and then another switch — to Cadillacs.
The first Caddy was maroon with a gray leatherette top,
followed by light gray with a navy top,
and finally, retired in Daytona Beach,
a black Cadillac convertible,
too darn hot in the sunshine,
but with AC available for the summer months.

My dad bought and sold cars, too,
for the fun of it, at a small corner dealership in Camp Hill,
driving down for the suburban Maryland car sale.
He drove each way, windows down,
Lucky smoldering in the ashtray.

Spring Day on 8th Street
- with thanks to Recluse-Poet of Orphan Mountain

My talent
won't compare
with Stafford's.
But writing poems
on Thursday afternoon
is worth a try.

In spring mist
geese fly over, geese fly over.
The courthouse clock
chimes mid-afternoon,
halfway to dusk.
School children, their teachers too,
count days until the Equinox.
For now the moon,
A partially filled saucer,
is witness to daffodil &
fragrant forsythia.
In wet light
small stones shine.

A good thing
people carry umbrellas,
wear Wellies,
walk near the river,
become poets.

Equinox

A room.
At dusk.
The leaves make black lace
against the sky.

The clock marks its
passing seconds.

She is concerned
about the President,
his leaning toward the future,
what's been abandoned.

News story a continent away,
in Newark,
a brick building, boarded,
uninhabitable.

Beneath night's cover,
a boy tags the back entrance
with neon paint.

"Ray lived here."

Umatilla Outflow
- The Land is my teacher.
             James Lavadour

In the nine-patch grid a Plateau star
        appears in red and white, at the center
                a penny-sized moon held by foggy sky.

The horizon shifts and tilts in cobalt,
        then magenta, puce, sunspot. Above Blue
                Mountain sediment, stillness at the center.

A forest burns – black skeleton trees,
        sooty smoke, orange flame. The triptych hollow,
                a fiery blaze of fractured upheaval.

Frost silences the world from the far ridge
        to foreground boulders. White mica reveals,
                conceals a safe location — mountain storehouse.

Rock and river, tide, sky, and memory—
        compounded along with Coltrane,
                the physicist's flow, and fingering instability.

The past laid open as evidence, traces of movement,
        infinite moment, what's there, balanced by
                the spirit of what's not.

Returning to the panels, their jewel-like color—
        wiping, raking, layering — she remembers *her* river,
                what the paintings say.

Begins With Seeing

Weekend morning, conversation at small tables,
    pastel landscapes on the wall,
        Army recruiter with a cup-to-go.

The wealthiest country in the world
    cajoles its citizens to read, funds studies
        that prove the ice caps are melting.

In Gallery 19 small rows of ancient
    Chinese ceramics, assembled & named:
        "Blue Parade" "Trail with Pale Bowls"

Boxes stacked in a dusty upstairs hallway,
    Paleo-flora – Proterozoic conifer & fossils
        from Wyoming – wait to be unwrapped.

In the West Wing with Turner – bravura brushwork,
    elemental forces, light's mystical bent –
        painting the sublime, eyes open.

In the East Wing the realist Hopper paints Maine,
    sky shadows, hills and houses.
        "Light at Two Lights" "Chop Suey" "Gas."

Juncos in the roses, pedestrians on the sidewalk:
    negotiated detail, tangles with what's lost.
        The Master reminds: *Make a way out of no way.*

What Do We Know

Across the living room a friend's glasses catch the light. She's holding her arms in front of her body, praying hands separated like book ends, about twelve inches apart. She's explaining the "All is one" idea behind Zeno's Paradoxes. "There is only now," she says, "this moment, and it does not change." Then she snaps her fingers and moves her hands to the right, "and then this moment, also unchanging." I stare in counterintuitive silence taking in the framed, unchanging snapshot of a moment, the Now the Buddhists speak of, the position of the subsurface rocks captured in a photograph of moving water, this second's immutable infinity.

The Pyrenees cheese we had at lunch, the story about a Carlton College interview, the lunchtime strawberries, the empty dessert plates carried from the room. What of them? The ex-moments and objects that reappear at will and clatter about in memory? If I think of them now, are they fractal-ed into the present along with everything else. St. Augustine said that his mind was on fire to understand the intricate riddles. Mary Oliver says, "I look and wonder, like everyone else." Here in an illuminated living room, watercolor in process angled on the drawing board, I think of timelines and post-it notes for following my own life's moments. I hold up my hands, snap the fingers of "Now."

Highway 26, Revisited

In love's sanctuary,
Thou art with me.
Eliza Gilkyson

Neon mosses
Gray, rain-pocked snow
Quartz Creek
Log trucks
and beach-goers driving Audis
Humboldt Mountain
Clatsop Forest
Lights On Thru Tunnels
Timber Trading Post – Closed for Winter
Camp 18
Old Growth Fir
Trucks-Enter-Road-Ahead
After the final set of outlet stores,
after the first chance you have to head
SW to Tillamook,
Ecola State Park beach
Haystack Rocks
the gray-green Pacific.

I Want To Say
after a poem by Natalie Goldberg,
at Hillcrest School for Girls

Before I am lost to time and to Hillcrest,
I want to say I was here.

I noticed the emerald hills, the red-brick
and wire, the pond with a blue spiral path.

I want you to know before I leave that the gray sky
here is the same sky above Oak Creek.

I wondered about the blue tape, the red tape, how any
stranger might feel in these halls of averted eyes.

I came to accept my position here,
fell in love with light framed by classroom windows.

Let me say, I felt the pain and irritation, suspected there was
kindness hidden, hoarded, counted, tucked-away.

I remember the afternoon Mrs. Foresee modeled 'paroxysym.'
I am thankful for that perfect circle where everyone wrote

and shared, true and extraordinary "I'm From" poems,
the ones we could have published right on-the-spot.

Before I leave this small, secluded world, I want to remind you:
With each breath you say No or Yes to your life,

the only life you get. I read the Library poster, the one which
proclaimed "Optimism." And then I looked for it. Listened hard.

I ate Jolly Ranchers, awarded for bringing my notebook,
and grapes shared by the school secretary.

I valued the quiet, pens and pencils moving along,
minds un-spooling onto empty notebook pages.

Wherever I go, I'll remember your sweatshirts and silliness,
longing, harsh laughter, stories — the families you hope to return to.

Change of Season
The stars
have already opened
their autumn eyes

Koyo

Sun-luscious afternoon in the park, she walks
the circles clockwise, then counter clockwise.

Late roses bloom, children slide and shout,
vermillion leaves prepare to obey gravity.

Across town a woman mourns her sister,
the many stages of grief appearing at once.

Another begins a job in Seattle,
says her colleagues seem "sane and, maybe, kind."

In reflected warmth, a Calico stretches
near the entrance to the old church.

Moss reappears, fluorescent green, outlining
the red bricks where locust leaves drift and dance.

You're older now, she thinks, *noticing more –*
the near and faraway – the invisible.

May 15th

It's not a test, but it *is* twenty-two springs ago,
a day not unlike this one – cool and wet, breaking
toward sun, and a few details we remember with
hazy certainty: Susan & Sabra smoking on the porch;
Mother's navy Georgette dress,
a room full of spring presents that took our breath away;
Judy Howard's watercolors,
including the table with a vase of daffodils;
our lost friends & those who remain;
Bill and Betty, whom we wish we'd invited,
Aunt Anne's champagne blessing,
saying our heart-felt vows, your final line:
"I am happy to be marrying you — at last!"

It is a long time ago *that* day,
and truly I miss my youthful self, before silver ,
the passionate, bright years that led us to May.
What's come after seems more like a roller-coaster,
a meander through both friendly countryside and hostile lands,
a river trip with challenges and bad weather.

These days you kiss my shin, check on sleep,
know my heart and its workings – completely,
perhaps at a frightful cost to your own heart.
But here we are, after a tile-store afternoon,
a vase of peonies, a drive out to Yamhill County.
Then one more Sunday morning with coffee,
The Oregonian, plus Robert Shuman for viola and piano.
A 22 year duet, that's what this has been, will be.
And I, your grateful, listening, loving — partner.

Abundant Heart
- at Shotpouch

Because the trees flowered, the nettles stung,
the grasses shone – July.

Because the table held asparagus, deviled eggs,
blue cheese and berry pie – the guests.

Because he said, "They should be complex and verdant" – the poems.

Because the creek flows west – the sunset.

Another Truth About Red Trees
- with thanks to Mark Allison

Sweet fires, elegy to summer's long goodbye,
you know them from the east side of the Alleghenies
Maple and Oak burnished by October's flinty light.

They remind you of bronzed baby shoes, first crocus,
haunted Mars, blood count afterimage,
river water shimmering with late light —
unstoppable beauty, particular-and-everyday at once,
accidental signals, ballast for any doubt or regret you carry.

Red trees in the west now, Japanese maple sentinels, curbside,
that Big Leaf out along Decker Road nestled near conifer green,
and in the blurred periphery driving north past Ash Creek swale.

The red trees remind you of the girl who drove west in her VW,
who picked-up hitchhikers and delivered them to hometowns
and homes in Clear Lake, Huntington, Ava.
And stories heard while the Moon Shadow followed
some day-blind star visible only from the Pacific rim.

Red trees. That girl. Fierce and sure,
the one who tracked down fear, surprised herself,
quilted another life, who kept on listening.

Today the trees signal autumn, its early, damp darkness,
wood-fire smoke in the neighborhood,
apples ripening in fruit-room baskets.
The painter set them down in acrylic;
the writer transforms them one more time.

Winter Listening

1.

It's Tuesday late, and blue-black night
sits silent, half-filled, almost as dazzling

as sun-bright day, almost as hopeful.
My resting body opens inside a breath; un-

focused moments reappear like backyard swallows;
Is it possible these flying fragments are a flock. The note

I didn't write yesterday, or a year ago, maybe
balanced by two airmail apologies to Iowa.

The furnace sends its wind-rush of heat
to hold off Arctic cold, welcome confetti stars.

New glasses, worn heart, my laconic angel
checks in when she damn-well pleases.

Day almost disappeared, words come,
smooth, translucent ice on the white page.

2.

It's Sunday, and along with dark, snow-laden clouds
narrow shafts of sunlight, almost as surprising

as the first side-yard crocus, almost as hopeful.
My body, mid-afternoon, transported,

softened by the sounds of geese
and Jasmine Orange tea. The call

I didn't make yesterday, no more plausible
than the poem I've been writing in my sleep.

The haughty angels loiter and frown.
The train passes through the city remembering

its return & the empty house out along
the Millersburg track. At the dining table,

candle light, tea, and apple pie,
Paradise recognizable as soon as you get there.

Sweet Dreams Baby
for the Sirens
in response to a poem in **The New Yorker**

In December
the nightingale will sing his song.
We'll tie ourselves to the masts,
six of them,
one for each of us.
One made from white pine,
one from a Brazilian hardwood,
one cherry, one maple, one oak, a yew.

Choose your masts, Sirens.
A handsome nightingale has promised,
I want to love you.
I am the Atlas to your soul.
And, *the sky is the listener.*
Composing new song after new song,
asking only,
How long from if, to will, to was?

The stars have disappeared in our late autumn sky.
These words erase pain, love,
mis-understanding.
No stones for this nightingale who takes flight.

Any singer can defeat me at my song,
an alto who sings descant and hopes
to return as a cello, as Yo Yo Ma's cello,
as Etta James, or back-up for Roy,
Sweet dreams baby, gottcha' dreaming sweet dreams,
the whole night through.

The universe is not without its art.
These fractaled selves
we see and see again.
Redbird made me a listener.
In Bahia I lost to songs of joy.
Tell me how I will be remembered.

Studies
- *for Paige*

1.

The Buddha says, *Make of yourself a light,*
and the painter wonders, *Which kind–*
visible or invisible?
Might she be, simply, the sensation of perceiving.
an illumination, a source, a signal.
Should she be a light that provides information,
a source of fire or of spiritual awareness.
The Buddha seems to say, *Choose one thing.*
but the artist's mind has a predilection for the numinous,
        the tangential.

2.

She works beside a luminary, but is not a shadow.
She lives with her own choice of standards –
the study of rivers and clouds, August, water.
She is a passenger too,
a certain enlivened expression in her eyes,
        animate laughter.

3.

Although the painter is not doctrinal in any way,
she remembers the Quaker Doctrine about
the unquestionable and guiding spirit in each person.
She accepts this, of course,
recognizes this light in her families, in children,
in that back-east landscape she left years ago.
When the painter sees something for the first time,
she sees one more fragment becoming
        part of the whole.

Winter Light

I have learned the litany of my life,
the pattern of repetitions, responsibilities,
and delights.

I have learned more than I ever
wanted to know, dream
        back into innocence,
life clean of regret, the sky cloudless.

Yet today reels me in
        and what remains –
        a crumb on the cutting-board, the rain-glazed cherry tree
        in a neighbor's garden, pale winter light –
        is cause for celebration.

Even my hungry mouth
cannot ask for more than this –
my heart beating in its cage,
my hands opening.

Saturday on the Glittering Strand

Another day of rain, the news cycle, interrupted sleep,
fence-post sentinels out along the property line.

In the teaching dream, restless girls at cafeteria tables
struggle at their seats, choose pencils, cannot write.

The teacher hoped for unstoppable words, daily journals
turned into memos and letters, poems, commandments.

Rusted-out red Saab, front tire flattened,
veers toward the lawyer's driveway.

Crumbs on the breadboard, blue grass banjo riff
Ralph Stanley croons, "Which road will you take?"

Hillary, recession, the endless war.
Can some new leader turn sails toward calm seas?

The list is mutable, detail after detail. Following the
poet's example, she makes *a parachute of all that is broken.*

Sappho's Latest
(For you) *the fragrant-bloomed Muses' lovely gifts*

Twenty-six centuries later we discover
another poem on papyrus used as cartonnage
for some long-dead Egyptian.
Twenty-six centuries later you make headlines,
in translation,
two Anglo Saxon men from Mars
try to figure your Venus-ian message.

Your latest has the usual accumulation of fragments:
Violet –yes! – hairturningwhite, fawn and lyre,
the old question of agelessness,
Tithonus & rose-armed Dawn,
the goddess wife who will bury the gray, aged man.

It is ever thus, Sappho,
men wondering what we mean,
what we care about,
even as they prepare for war.

You saw it all, they say,
and kept on with your poems on cloth:
Extant fragments
empty spaces awaiting bracketed conjectures,
enough mysterious language to ignite academy quarrels,
enough to make your reputation.

We wonder, from our comfortable living rooms,
pure water pouring from the tap,
with Thai take-out, electric lights, flypaper,
what it was that made you write —
and know
the answer is as simple as bloodthirsty Charlotte's:
Hunger, sex and light – now's attentive yearning –
some zealous instinct for the everlasting.

Reflection

Hope has summered over, Strawberry moon
rising over Oak Creek pasture,
dappled light dancing on the bedroom wall.

Back pain, then needles burning with *aiye*,
Demetrius and Laertes sleeping
while the chorus girls imagine the dawn.

In the dream she walks a meadow,
child again, deserving love.
Brooding shadows warn, "Be careful."

When she hears creek water spill over rock
she revises that caution, "Be full of care."

Singer

Satchel Full of Poems

You step inside with a satchel full of poems,
the one where red trees represent the girl you were,
the one with tides coming and going, the full moon.
Does it take seven years for sorrow to reach the soul?

Red trees represent the girl you were,
confident and sure, you headed west one summer.
They say it takes seven years for sorrow to reach the soul.
Now the trees signal autumn, its early damp darkness.

Confident and sure, you headed west one summer.
Apples ripening in fruit room baskets,
now the trees signal autumn, its early damp darkness.
Tenderly, let us recognize all kinds of memory.

Apples ripening in fruit room baskets,
our dreams are filled with whispering ghosts.
Tenderly, let us recognize all kinds of memory.
Nothing remains uncovered, not even dark clouds.

Our dreams are filled with whispering ghosts,
tides coming going, the full moon,
nothing remains uncovered, not even dark clouds.
You step inside with a satchel full of poems.

Recent Work
   "You know where I am ... "
   (Bill walking toward the easel)

I am the trees bending with night storm winds.
I am the wave breaking white, over rock.
I am the forest stump, wild morels
        and a Canyon Creek deadfall catching water's reflected light.
I am the nightscape and the blue boat on Clear Lake.
I am the deer haven and the deer.
I am the trail honoring Alan and someone walking there in spring
snow,
        the Metolius and its reflection.
I am the Ochoco summit and the Philomath landscape.
I am the fir cone and branch with moss.
I am the ravine where Spring Creek runs wet and runs dry,
        and Spring Creek again and again.
I am the crow and the starling ("Oh! No!")
I am Peterson's at 3 am and 3 am with wind-blown leaves.
I am the invisible night stars, the lunar eclipse,
        the moon itself and the shadow of earth covering it.
I am the whole dream of these things.

You see, I am alive, I am alive, I am alive.

                    with thanks to N. Scott Momaday

Four Floors Up, Pen In Hand

Find the evidence of those before you,
*   listen for the sound of your heart.*

We settle in
quiet, thoughtful, exuberant.
Across the way Mary fills up pages,
beside Pat an empty chair waits for Laura.
Computer keys clicking – rush of Anne's words.
Kate smiles as her pen moves along.
Everyone leans into a notebook.
Outside the air is cool,
three kinds of gray clouds layered over the city,
another season.
Whooshing traffic on Burnside,
a car radio plays country,
a train, a flock of birds,
some plaintive voice somewhere,
but on the bright blue table we're writing along,
munching pretzels, reaching for strawberries Scott offers.
A plastic bag is untied - sesame scent.
"*Arrivederci*" I write, remembering Jessica's taxi driver,
then a house from my childhood –
gray clapboard siding, red brick chimney –
tides coming and going, the full moon.
We are writing memoir, but there is only Now,
followed by Now,
and this is why the past is not only not dead,
but is never past.
We trust these empty pages,
stories, songs and dreams unspooling.
Pale blue lines accept what comes.

Valentine for Steve

You know
you're more than
an occasional lover –
of poetry –
when a few words
taken from
a part
of
a poem
remind you
of another poem.
["Let everyone learn how to whistle."
connects
directly
in my case,
to
"Reasons for Loving a Harmonica,"
another poem
I have mined over
& over again,
as a prompt,
as a starting spot,
as in,
"Reasons to Love Your Cat"
"Reasons to Wonder About Stars"
"Reasons to Consider Rain"]
And, as is usual,
my friend
has
not only
bought the gingerbread
and two forks,
divided it =ly
splitting the calories
and the lemon icing,

but also
found this prompt,
ostensibly
about
learning to whistle,
covertly
about
how to be
a friend.

Upwelling

Out along Shotpouch, water rilling over rock,
air cool and damp, mud-pathed glory of larkspur,

Late May sunshine arrives,
hazel leaf-shadows dance with the wind.

Star whites emerge among canary grasses,
blackberries barb through cotton gloves,

Bees buzz by the sword fern, distant chain saw,
murmur of voices from the Sacred Cedar Trail.

I say to myself, this day dazzles like no other,
this day obliterates news headlines,

the pain inside a morning kitchen.
Working near the cabin Franz made,

among the thirty thousand trees he planted,
there is only stillness, there is only Now.

Corvid
- *In substance, I side with the crow.*

Raucous caw-caw-cawing
       & jet plumage glossed with sunlit purple
            announce your neighborly presence.

Wary opportunist, indifferent and comfortable,
       funny fool-arounder with a three-foot wingspread,
            you are as universal as the eye of god.

You survey the dunes, and mown-grass fields,
       cruise parking lots, the landfill, the front yard,
            scavenge for displaced grasshoppers,

mice, waste grain, golf balls & old shoelaces.
       Your spring home a humble bowl of sticks
            in the high fork of a tree – eggs, green-spotted.

After nesting season the gang gathers,
       commuting from miles around
            to roost in the old poplars on 8th Street.

From the trees' high perch, from the garage roofline,
       you watch our comings and goings,
            the folly of those who no longer fly.

In Praise of Walking Around
  - with gratitude, for Pablo Neruda

It happens that I am tired of being a woman,
It happens that I am tired of going into Nordstrom's
          and the cineplex
all dolled-up, available, like a felt giraffe
swimming in waters of salt and tears.

Skeins of woolen yarn make me weep.
I want nothing but the arising of either poppy or peony.
I want to see no more armories, no more gun shops
nor outlets nor strip malls.

It happens that I am tired of my smile, and my hands
and my dreams and my shadow.
It happens that I am tired of being a woman.

Just the same it would be delightful
to scare the postman or the meter-reader.

It would be fanciful
to go through the cemetery with lighted candles
whispering until I burst into flame.

I do not want to go on being ice,
fog hugging low water and dissipating dreams, sleepless.
I do not want to go on thinking every night.

I do not want to be the inheritor of so many things.
I do not want to continue as a rock, as a tomb
as a solitary stream, as a reservoir filled with fish
cold and dying in the rain.

For this reason, Thursday burns like gasoline
at the sight of me arriving with my teacher face.
And the day caws in passing like a solo crow,
the day's footsteps toward daylight are filled with hope.

And the day shoves me along to particular corners,
                particular rooms,
to cathedrals where bones frame the windows,
to a particular cafe smelling of cinnamon,
to streets, frightening as mines.

There are insects the color of tangerines and wreathes hanging
                from the doors of houses which I hate.
There are forgotten shoes in cardboard boxes.

There are mirrors
which might have wept or crowed with joy,
there are mittens all over the place, and lullabies and poems.
I move along, inquisitive, with eyes,
with memories, with regrets.
I review. I pass offices full of machines
and courtyards hung with baskets of fuscia,
a stained table square, yellow towels
which cry out and weep.

Catching the Light,
and Therefore, the Shadows
- for Ralph, the photographer

It's a road you've never been on, or one you passed by in eastern Wyoming the summer of 1970.

Or Tioga Road in West Virginia, where Cathy, her granddad and the black Spaniel cruised, coal sparkling on the flat-topped mountains.

Or maybe the soft green curve of the Pennsylvania Turnpike you dreamed the night you decided you'd never go back.

Or Linglestown Road, headed east after swim practice, summer stretched out ahead of you forever.

But this road is for walking, no sound but an occasional daylight call, flash of Scrub-jay, water sound in the distance.

Could this be the road along Pine Creek, green-black water scrambling over granite, filling the quarry.

Or that back-road outside State College where you picnicked in a field of Tansy ragwort before graduation.

Or, decades later, the grassy spot where you abandoned the Honda and walked downhill to Drift Creek, heard Jeff "call the owls in."

But, of course, this road is the photographer's, west side of the Coast Range, where he discovers himself again and again.

Primary Sources

The river's primary source is rain,
The rains' primary sources are the clouds.
The primary source of clouds is the molecule.
The primary source of the molecule is the atom.
Atoms are the primary sources of all elements.
The primary source of the poem is the rhythm of the line
        or that opening word.
The poem's seed is the dream of the Dream of Now.
Now has no source, it just is.
Now is itself, alone, singular – now past.
The primary source of the future is the empty line below this one.

In this room one woman is planning her wedding.
Two men are discussing art.
One man half-heartedly browses a book about God,
and seven plan a Peace Walk.
Two women are noticing, writing it down.

There Are So Many Hegelians
- after Robert Bly

The geese insist there is only one way.
The nail that penetrated your hand has been removed.
Eight crows hunt for seed in the mud.

An eyelash moon arises in the west.
There is one Burning Heart and so many Hegelians.
The morning star is hidden behind overcast gray.

To those who wake up and make music
I say: Your task is to sing for the voiceless,
to remember the cry that becomes song.

Probably we *were* born too near the heat,
and like the fire, we have dancing flames.
A touch, a voice across the wire, sizzles.

There are more clouds than have ever been named.
They move, cast shadows, are dazzled by light.
Some people say a photograph is a vessel of Now.

Some words are just right in this poem, Ann,
Though Stafford could do it better,
you are the one alive today.

Job Description
- for the apprentices

Be nourishing as damp spring soil,
tenacious, faithful as seed buried there.
Be quick, clear as water in a freshet,
determined to go the distance to the sea.
Be solid, dependable as river rock,
smooth and malleable to stream flow.
Have a preference for order &
the ability to laugh during chaos.
Whisper to the bully,
"I don't want to crush your spirit,"
to the shy, self-conscious one,
"I love your socks."
In a world of straight rows
facing the chalkboard, intercom, flag,
make a circle, listen, sit near the light.
Magician, custodian, queen and scholar,
remember when you learned to speak Portuguese,
remember the play – no part for you –
Remember the loneliness of the beginner's path,
and be a beginner again –
and again – because you are, will be,
with each new circle, in every lighted space.
Be the ladder, be the lighthouse,
be the lightning bug.
Be the open heart, an idea unspooling.
Be the teacher you needed
that winter your grandfather died,
and the next year when you walked-on to Varsity.
Know yourself as essential,
your students, most important.
You will give and give and give.
No one will witness
your six hundred close judgment calls a day,
but your students will remember
notes in your handwriting
written in the margins of their young lives.

So Much Silence
  - with thanks to Robert Bly

Tell me why it is that March is filled with loneliness,
that we're not out in the streets crying or raging
about the three wars, the melting ice caps.

I say to myself, *Go on and cry, rage,*
if it helps you take a deep breath or
feel the surprise of forsythia's golden reach.

We will all have to solve the riddle of corporate personhood,
of Hamlet's Blackberry. Our angels are on disability;
they're not crossing the picket lines either.

Have we agreed to so many wars, to so much silence
or does the way of the empty branch reveal
the structure and the sky, too?

We've listened to the great singers:
Whitman, Akhmatova, Emerson, Dickinson.
Still we are afraid to sing solo and in harmony.

Some Masters say our life lasts
only seven days, or a season.
Is it already Tuesday, Ann, has winter ended?

Singer
- with thanks to Robert Bly

I have spent my whole life remembering,
Honor the brown winter wren who searches for food.
Here I am singing along with Emmy Lou and Patty.

My talent amounts to persistence in following
moving water. Sometimes the rills and the meander
show us the heart of the way.

Thank the goddesses for Sappho who left us her fragmented
love poems. We are timid; we have been beaten back,
but water moves rock one grain at a time.

It was only when I paid attention
to the voices in my dreams that I
understood what the blue door might mean.

I don't think you've ever heard the nightengale's
rare song. He is like the poet Hafiz
repeating the words of his Beloved, Shams of Tabriz.

I hope you're not hiding in this poem, Ann.
You don't always need Stafford or Oliver.
We're just talking words here–disappearing in water and wind.

What Next

She wakes in dark night to emptiness. She suspects
the next frightening step might be fullness.

Her father dies. After the rosary
she feels herself a passenger on a slow-moving train.

Grinding rose quartz and cobalt, she paints a
10th century Madonna — brings a lavender offering.

In rooms filled with strangers she wonders what to speak of:
Nietzsche, her dream of bursting into flame, the tuna salad.

Looking across a table of pamphlets and petitions he announces,
"I have in my garage the history of the old lumberyard."

At the reading he forgets to honor the dead poet
but his stories make everyone laugh.

Thirty-five miles up the Methow River she remembers
the words of Sappho: *What cannot be said will be wept.*

About Ann Staley:

Ann Staley knew she wanted to be a teacher by 2nd grade and a writer by 4th grade, when her mother gave her stationery with her name printed across the top in red lettering. She grew up in the Keystone State and migrated west in her white 1961 VW bug called "Moon Shadow." At the time she was reading Tom Wolfe's non-fiction and Kurt Vonnegut's fiction plus teaching herself to play the autoharp. In order to proclaim full independence, and to get away from an ex-husband, she knew she needed to get "as far away from her roots" as was possible. When the Golden Gate Bridge led her to Pacific Highway 101 she turned right and drove north to Oregon. She took the Smith River Highway from the coast to the Rogue Valley, then headed south toward Ashland where she had, in her address book, the names of people she'd never met. In this way she found herself nineteen miles up the Green Springs Highway, living in a small cabin with a wood stove. She wrote terrible poetry that year including an autobiography she sent as her letter of introduction while she looked for her first teaching position in southern Oregon.

Forty years later, a retired teacher who has taught everyone from grandmothers and fifth-graders right on through graduate school, Ann likes nothing better than settling into a circle of strangers-becoming-friends, opening her notebook and saying, "Let's do some freewriting for a few minutes before our introductions. Write about whatever comes to mind. Write yourself into this room, leaving behind your to-do lists and regrets. There is only Now followed by Now."

Ann has degrees from Pennsylvania State University, Southern Oregon University, and Stanford University. She has taught in five Oregon school districts, in two community colleges, and in two public universities and two private ones. On her tombstone she wants the following engraved: "Loved this world, pen in hand."

CPSIA information can be obtained at www.ICGtesting.com
Printed in the USA
BVOW041517200911

271492BV00001B/7/P

9 781935 961239